BEANS

BEANS

W. PARK KERR

William Morrow and Company, Inc.

New York

A million thanks to Harriet Bell, editor; Louise Fili, designer; Betty Alfenito, prop stylist; Anne Disrude, food stylist; Ellen Silverman, photographer; Janice Faber and Virginia Mayo, assistants

To Jonny Rogers, the true definition of friendship

Introduction

❋

BEANS HAVE UNDERGONE A CULINARY MAKEOVER, MAKING THOSE HUMAN FASHION MAKEOVERS on television seem lackluster by comparison. Beans, once considered peasant food, are now glamorized on the covers of food magazines and prominently displayed in chic bags on gourmet market shelves.

What caused the public to finally recognize the lowly but versatile bean as a candidate for culinary stardom? First, cooks got off their high horses about haute cuisine and admitted that simple food tastes great. Beans have always been known as "the meat of the masses." Many cooks instinctively knew that if they combined beans with grains or a little meat, the protein in each food would complement the other, and their entire protein intake would be increased. Beans, therefore, form the backbone of many food cultures, and the increased popularity of ethnic foods also brought beans out of the supporting cast into the spotlight.

Cooks also began paying more attention to healthier foods, and beans are certainly one of the best-tasting, healthiest foods you can put in a pot. They're high in complex carbohydrates, protein, and fiber, full of iron and B vitamins, and (with very few exceptions) low in fat and calories.

Finally, people love new foods. A bean shopper expecting to find the usual suspects—garbanzos, pintos, great Northerns, and the like—is now offered an array of unfamiliar beans with intriguing names that sound more like rock groups than legumes: calypsos, scarlet runners, tongues-of-fire, rattlesnakes. While these beans are not exactly new (they were old heirloom varieties that savvy farmers rediscovered and planted to meet legume lovers' demands), they spark the cook's imagination, and a new kind of "jumping beans" was discovered—the kind that jump off the market shelves and into shopping carts. There are more than fourteen thousand kinds of legumes, the edible mature seeds inside pod-bearing plants, so even the most avid bean fan has plenty of beans to discover.

It wasn't so long ago that beans were mainly considered in America as just something that was spooned onto your plate as a side dish to the meat course—refried beans with an enchilada, baked beans with the spareribs. Now, beans are all over the menu. They can be found making up a spicy bean dip for crunchy tortillas, enlivening a green salad, or even starring as the main attraction. To me, beans are best when cooked the southwestern way, with plenty of garlic, chiles, onions, and olive oil, and this book gives my favorite recipes for these newly appreciated darlings of the kitchen. So, go ahead and say that I'm full of beans—I consider it a compliment.

Avocado-Chickpea Spread

✤

MAKES ABOUT 3 CUPS

A HAPPY MARRIAGE BETWEEN TWO STARS OF THE COCKTAIL PARTY DIP CIRCUIT, GUACAMOLE AND HUMMUS, this smooth green spread has a passle of possibilities—slathered onto Garlic Pita Crisps, served with crunchy homemade Tostaditas (page 57) as a dip, or stuffed into pita bread as a vegetarian sandwich filling.

3 cups cooked and drained chickpeas
2 California avocados, pitted and peeled
1/3 cup olive oil
1/3 cup fresh lime juice
4 garlic cloves, peeled and chopped
1 3/4 teaspoons ground cumin,
  preferably from toasted seeds (page 38)

1 1/2 teaspoons salt
1 1/4 teaspoons freshly ground black pepper
2 tablespoons minced cilantro, mint, or
  parsley, or a mixture of all three,
  for garnish
12 tomatillos or cherry tomatoes
Garlic Pita Crisps (page 54)

In a food processor, combine everything but the garnish herbs, tomatillos, and pita crisps. Process until smooth, stopping to scrape down the sides of the work bowl once or twice. Adjust the seasoning. *(The spread can be prepared 1 day in advance of serving. Cover tightly with plastic wrap and refrigerate. Return to room temperature before serving.)*

Mound the spread in the middle of a platter, sprinkle it with the herbs, surround it with the cherry tomatoes and pita crisps, and serve it immediately.

Chunky Three-Bean Salsa

❋

PICK JUST ABOUT ANY THREE COOKED DRIED BEANS (CHOOSE THEM FOR CONTRAST IN COLOR AND TEXTURE), prepared in just about any manner (freshly cooked or canned), and mix them up to make this bumpy-textured salsa. It doesn't take much to figure out how fabulous this is on a tostadita, but serve it as a relish for a thick grilled steak for a real bull's-eye.

2 cups chunky tomato-based hot salsa
1 cup cooked and drained black-eyed peas
1 cup cooked and drained baby lima beans
1 cup cooked and drained dark red
   kidney beans

1 large heavy sweet red pepper, roasted, peeled, and diced (page 41)
3 long green chiles, roasted, peeled, and diced (page 41), or ½ cup frozen chopped green chiles, thawed and drained
⅓ cup finely chopped cilantro

In a medium bowl, stir together all the ingredients except the cilantro. Cover and refrigerate for at least 1 hour. *(The salsa can be prepared up to 3 days ahead.)*

Return the salsa to room temperature. Stir in the cilantro and serve, accompanied by tostaditas.

Fiesta Black Bean Dip

THERE ARE MORE BEAN DIPS OUT THERE THAN FLIES ON A HEIFER, BUT FEW OF THEM ARE AS GOOD AS THIS ONE. Chorizo sausage, chipotles en adobo, and roasted garlic are three ingredients that separate it from the herd.

4 whole unpeeled garlic cloves
¼ cup olive oil
½ pound chorizo
3 cups cooked and drained black beans
1 ⅓ cups lightly salted chicken broth
3 canned chipotles en adobo, plus 1 to 2
　teaspoons sauce from the can

½ pound grated Monterey Jack or
　Cheddar cheese, or a combination of both
6 green onions, trimmed and thinly sliced
Tostaditas, homemade (page 57)
　or purchased

Position a rack in the middle of the oven and preheat to 375°F. In a small oven-proof bowl, combine the garlic and olive oil. Bake the garlic, uncovered, basting the cloves occasionally with the oil, until very soft, about 20 minutes.

Cool to room temperature. Squeeze the garlic cloves out of their peels; reserve the oil and softened garlic.

Crumble the chorizo into a cold skillet, set it over medium heat, and cook, stirring, until lightly browned, about 10 minutes. With a slotted spoon, transfer the sausage to paper towels to drain.

In a food processor, combine the beans, broth, garlic cloves, their oil, and the chipotles and their sauce and process until fairly smooth. Transfer the purée to a heavy, preferably nonstick saucepan and set it over low heat. Add the chorizo and cook, partially covered, stirring often, until thick, about 10 minutes.

Divide the bean mixture between 2 wide, shallow bowls. Sprinkle the cheese evenly over the 2 bowls, scatter the green onions over the cheese, and serve immediately, accompanied by the tostaditas.

Bean Bagging: Buying and Storing Dried Beans

✵

DRIED BEANS ARE VIRTUALLY IMMORTAL, HAVING REMAINED EDIBLE (THAT IS, COOKABLE AND EVEN GROWABLE) for hundreds of years. Although some bean-*meisters* warn buyers to purchase the freshest beans available from a reputable source with a high turnover, that advice is really just a lot of culinary hogwash. True, you don't know exactly how old the beans in the supermarket are, but it is no big deal. If they are long in the tooth and have dehydrated even more since the day they were packed, the beans will just take a little longer to cook to tenderness.

It's more important that the beans be clean, as little clods of dirt and stone often find their way into the packages. Inexpensive bulk beans from a bin in a health food or discount store have a special tendency toward this problem. Those pricey little bags of boutique or heirloom beans, in my experience (and I have seen a hill of beans over the years), seem to have been impeccably sorted and cleaned, helping to justify their high prices. Like the age question, bean cleanliness is no big deal. Before cooking any dried beans, always sort through them, looking for mismatched or misshapen beans and pebbles or soil. To help the search mission, pour dark beans onto a light-colored surface and vice versa. (Give the expensive beans a perfunctory sorting too.)

Store beans airtight at room temperature. I display them in glass jars, the better to enjoy their colors and markings. Try to use them up in a reasonable amount of time (say, 6 months or so), but don't throw out older beans: soaked overnight with a generous covering of cold water, then leisurely simmered in fresh water, they should be just fine.

Freezing Beans; Frozen Beans

DRIED BEANS THAT HAVE BEEN SOAKED AND SIMMERED CAN BE SUCCESSFULLY FROZEN FOR FUTURE USE. Put them up in small plastic containers, covered with their cooking water. Thaw at room temperature; drain and rinse before using.

Frozen beans (commonly black-eyed peas, lima beans, and baby limas) can be quite successful and certainly taste better than canned beans. Depending on the brand, they may need a brief simmer in unsalted water. Thaw the beans and taste several to determine how crunchy they are; cook accordingly, depending on the use you have for them.

Canned Beans

CANNED BEANS ARE A GREAT CONVENIENCE, ALTHOUGH THE CANNING PROCESS TENDS TO HOMOGENIZE THE BEANS, removing their individual character. Some brands are better than others in producing beans that are large, firm, colorful, and fresher-tasting; shop around. Drain the beans and rinse them briefly to remove the canning liquid. One 16-ounce can of beans (a common size) will yield about 1 1/2 cups drained, rinsed beans.

Quick-Soaking Dried Beans

MOST BEANS ARE FULLY REHYDRATED AFTER ONLY 4 HOURS OF SOAKING, but in an emergency you can quick-soak beans using this method: After sorting and rinsing, place the beans in a large heavy pan and cover with tepid unsalted water. Set over medium heat and bring to a simmer, uncovered. Simmer for 1 minute. Remove the beans from the heat, cover the pan, and let stand on a rack until the beans are cool, about 1 hour. Drain the beans and proceed as if they had been soaked for the full length of time.

Cooking Dried Beans

❋

To SOAK OR NOT TO SOAK, THAT IS THE BEAN LOVER'S DILEMMA. ONLY DRIED SPLIT PEAS AND LENTILS do not need to be rehydrated, so the controversy must be addressed with all the other bean varieties. The anti-soaking contingency argues that soaking reduces the beans' flavor somewhat, is time-consuming, and may not improve the beans' digestibility (the big reason the pro-soakers soak their beans). I'm a pro-soaker. Soaked beans cook much more evenly, are less prone to split, and if there is any chance that soaking does reduce the gas-causing sugars found in beans, I say it's worth the extra step. (Fiber in beans also plays a part in the bean digestibility problem, and you can't reduce the fiber.) Besides, how hard is it to cover a pot of beans with water and let it sit for 4 hours before cooking?

Yes, only 4 hours, not overnight. Most cooks cling to the old-fashioned premise that beans need to be soaked at least overnight before cooking. Nope—beans do not absorb significant water after that first 4 hours. The overnight soaking period is a convenience, not a requirement. To soak the beans, sort through them first, looking for foreign objects to discard, then rinse well under cold water and drain. Place them in a large bowl and add enough cold (or boiling) water to cover the beans by at least 2 inches. Let stand at room temperature for 4 hours (2 hours if you use boiling water), or longer, up to overnight, refrigerating the bowl of beans during warm weather. The "quick-soaking" method is popular—boiling the beans in a pot for 2 minutes, then covering and letting stand for 1 hour off the heat—but it often causes the beans to break up during cooking. Drain the beans, discarding the soaking water, which will contain some of the sugars that have leached out of the beans.

Place the drained beans in a large heavy-bottomed pot and add enough fresh water to cover them by at least 3 inches, leaving at least 2 inches of head space between the top of the water and the rim of the pot. Do not add salt. Both salt and acidic ingredients like molasses, ketchup, or tomatoes will keep the beans from tenderizing, and most of the recipes in this book are seasoned after the beans are cooked anyway. Bring the beans to a boil over medium heat. As soon as they reach a simmer, reduce the heat to very low. Cover the pan tightly and simmer gently until the beans are tender but still hold their shape. In general, all beans will take about 30 minutes to 1 1/2 hours to cook, but test them often by biting into a few—test more than one, as they do not always cook evenly. Do not mix different batches of dried beans because they never cook at the same rate. For the best texture, cool the beans in their liquid still in the pot and set on a rack. Store the cooked beans in their cooking liquid, covered and refrigerated, and drain just before using. The

cooking liquid usually thickens into a delicious sauce. One pound of dried beans, soaked and cooked, will yield 6 to 7 cups.

Canned beans are convenient, but the canning process tends to neutralize the special character of the individual bean variety, making them all a bit too similar in texture and flavor for my taste. Brands vary, with some canners more successful than others in producing beans that are large, firm, colorful, and fresh-tasting, so shop around. Before using, drain the beans and rinse them briefly under cold running water to remove the highly salty canning liquid. One 16-ounce can of beans (a common size, although you will find 15- and 19-ounce cans) will yield about $1\frac{1}{2}$ cups drained, rinsed beans.

Bean-Jeweled: Heirloom and Boutique Beans

GOOD NEWS FOR BEAN LOVERS! JUST WHEN YOU THOUGHT YOU HAD COOKED YOUR WAY THROUGH EVERY BAG OF BEANS at the supermarket, specialty food stores began stocking their shelves with a rainbow-like array of new bean varieties. It should only be a matter of time before these newcomers are stocked right alongside the old pintos, garbanzos, and red kidneys.

Produced by a few small growers, these unfamiliar beans fall into two general categories, heirloom and boutique. Heirloom beans, like the heirloom produce and flowers that are returning to the market, are old-fashioned varieties that fell from favor for one reason or another. Some of these beans were tricky to grow, while others just got forgotten in the rush to produce uniform food for the masses, but committed farmers are taking the time to bring them back. One long-lost heirloom bean was discovered in a sealed jar in a Kentucky cave and husbanded back to abundance by a single New Mexico grower. Jacob's cattle beans, also called Anasazi beans, are probably the most familiar of the heirloom beans. Boutique beans are either new hybrids, such as the rattlesnake bean, or foreign imports (or reimports, since many beans originated in the Americas), such as the flageolet.

Due to the demand by home cooks and restaurant chefs for the unusual and exotic, more and more of these beans are finding their way into the mainstream. Some of the beans are much tastier than their prosaic cousins, but all are at least as good, and most are prettier to look at. As in life, however, bean beauty can be fleeting—those colorful markings on the heirloom or boutique varieties that catch your eye at the market will often disappear during cooking. But flavor is the issue here: if you like everyday beans, you'll love heirloom or boutique beans.

Gingered Yellow Split Pea Soup with Cilantro Cream

MAKES 4 TO 6 SERVINGS

IN ITS USUAL GUISES, SPLIT PEA SOUP IS AS COMFORTING AND FAMILIAR AS A PAIR OF OLD SLIPPERS. This golden yellow version is uncommonly zesty, with fresh ginger, chile peppers, sweet carrots, and red bell peppers.

2 medium jalapeños, stemmed and chopped

1 3/4-inch cube peeled fresh ginger

3 garlic cloves, peeled and chopped

3 tablespoons olive oil

1 1/2 cups chopped yellow onions

3 medium carrots, peeled and chopped

2 teaspoons ground cumin, preferably from toasted seeds (page 38)

1 large heavy sweet red pepper, stemmed, seeded, and diced

1 1/2 cups yellow split peas, picked over and rinsed

5 1/2 cups lightly salted chicken broth

1 1/2 teaspoons salt

Cilantro Cream (recipe follows)

In a mini food processor, purée together the jalapeños, ginger, and garlic.

In a large soup pot over medium heat, warm the oil. Add the onions, carrots, jalapeño purée, and cumin and cook, covered, stirring once or twice, for 5 minutes. Stir in the sweet red pepper and cook, covered, for 5 minutes, stirring occasionally.

Add the split peas, broth, and salt and bring to a simmer, skimming occasionally. Partially cover the pan and cook, stirring occasionally, until the split peas are very tender and the soup is thick, about 40 minutes.

Remove from the heat and cool slightly. In a food processor, purée half the soup. Return the puréed soup to the pan. *(The soup can be prepared to this point up to 3 days in advance. Cool completely, cover, and refrigerate.)*

Rewarm the soup over low heat until steaming; adjust the seasoning. Ladle the soup into bowls. Drizzle the soup with the Cilantro Cream.

Cilantro Cream

1/2 cup Crema (page 57) or sour cream

1/3 cup finely chopped cilantro

Pinch of salt

Pinch of freshly ground black pepper

In a mini food processor, combine the crema, cilantro, salt, and pepper and process until smooth. *(The cream can be prepared up to 1 day ahead. Cover and refrigerate, returning it to room temperature before using.)*

Chickpea Soup with Grilled Sausages and Green Sage Oil

❋

START WITH A RICH, GOLDEN CHICKPEA PURÉE, TOP WITH SLICES OF YOUR FAVORITE GRILLED SAUSAGE (anything from mild sweet Italian to fiery Cajun andouille), and drizzle with pungent green sage oil.

3 tablespoons olive oil
1 ½ cups chopped yellow onions
1 cup chopped carrots
4 garlic cloves, peeled and minced
¼ teaspoon dried thyme, crumbled
1 bay leaf
3 cups cooked and drained chickpeas

4 ½ cups lightly salted chicken broth
½ teaspoon freshly ground black pepper
Salt
4 links (about 1 pound) best-quality pork
   sausage, grilled or broiled
Sage Oil (recipe follows)

Heat the oil in a medium saucepan. Add the onions, carrots, garlic, thyme, and bay leaf; cover and cook for 10 minutes, stirring occasionally.

Add the chickpeas, broth, and pepper and bring to a simmer. Cook, uncovered, until the vegetables are tender and the chickpeas are very tender, about 35 minutes.

Cool slightly. Discard the bay leaf and, working in batches, purée the soup in a food processor. (The soup can be prepared to this point a day or two in advance of serving. Cool completely and refrigerate.) Return the soup to the pan and rewarm it over low heat. Add salt to taste.

Thinly slice the sausages on the diagonal. Ladle the soup into wide bowls. Arrange the sausage slices over the surface of the soup. Drizzle the sage oil evenly over all and serve immediately.

Sage Oil

⅓ cup extra virgin olive oil   ¼ cup finely chopped fresh sage leaves   Pinch of salt

In a mini food processor, combine the oil, sage, and salt. Process until smooth. Let stand for 1 hour. Transfer the oil mixture to a fine strainer set over a bowl. Press with the back of a spoon to extract as much oil as possible. Discard the herb pulp. Use the oil immediately or refrigerate, returning it to room temperature when needed.

Hot and Smoky Bean-Corn Salad with Chile-Roasted Chicken

✻

Colorful and dramatic, this salad is the perfect main course for a warm summer evening's supper. Try to use the heirloom beans called tongues-of-fire, with their mottled brown skins.

3 ½ cups cooked and drained tongues-of-fire beans (or substitute cranberry or pinto beans)

1 ½ cups well-drained corn kernels, thawed or canned

1 heavy sweet red pepper, roasted, peeled, and diced (page 41)

½ cup thinly sliced green onions

4 teaspoons Dijon mustard

4 teaspoons red wine vinegar

2 teaspoons molasses

1 canned chipotle en adobo, minced, plus 2 teaspoons sauce from the can

¼ teaspoon salt

½ cup corn oil

Crisp inner leaves of romaine lettuce

1 Chile-Roasted Chicken (recipe follows), at room temperature and carved into serving pieces

In a large bowl, toss together the beans, corn, red pepper, and green onions. In a medium bowl, whisk together the mustard, vinegar, molasses, chipotle, chipotle sauce, and salt. Gradually whisk in the oil. Pour the dressing over the beans and toss. Adjust the seasoning.

Line 4 plates with leaves of romaine. Divide the bean salad over the lettuce. Top the salad with the chicken and serve immediately.

Chile-Roasted Chicken

3 ½-pound young roasting chicken

1 tablespoon olive oil

1 tablespoon unblended medium-hot powdered red chiles, preferably from Chimayo or Dixon, New Mexico

Salt

Preheat the oven to 400°F. Pat the chicken dry and set it on a rack in a shallow baking dish. Rub the chicken with the olive oil. Sprinkle the powdered chiles over the chicken and rub it into the skin. Season with a generous sprinkling of salt. Bake the chicken until the skin is crisply browned and a thigh, when pricked at its thickest part, yields pinkish-yellow juices, about 1 hour.

El Paso Red Beans and Rice

❋

MAKES 6 TO 8 SERVINGS

RED BEANS AND RICE, A CLASSIC CREOLE DISH, IS PRETTY
DARNED GOOD, but I think it can be made even better with a kick from some
powerful West Texas seasoning. If you can find it, use fresh chorizo sausage (not the
hard, smoked chorizo) instead of the more common hot Italian for authentic flavor.

1 pound hot Italian sausage, casings removed
2 cups chopped yellow onions
4 garlic cloves, peeled and minced
1 tablespoon unblended medium-hot
   powdered red chiles, preferably from
   Chimayo or Dixon, New Mexico
1 tablespoon dried oregano, crumbled
1 tablespoon ground cumin, preferably
   from toasted seeds (page 38)

7 cups cooked and drained red kidney beans
5 cups lightly salted chicken broth
1 cup canned crushed tomatoes in purée
4 teaspoons salt
6 long green chiles, roasted, peeled, and
   chopped (page 41), or 1 cup frozen
   chopped green chiles, thawed and drained
8 cups hot cooked white rice

Crumble the sausage into a heavy 5-quart pot. Set over low heat and cook, uncovered, breaking up the larger lumps of meat, until lightly browned, about 10 minutes.
With a slotted spoon, transfer the sausage to a bowl.

Return the pan to low heat. Add the onions, garlic, powdered chiles, oregano, and
cumin. Cover and cook, stirring often and scraping the bottom of the pan, for 10 minutes.
Add the beans, broth, tomatoes, and salt and bring to a simmer. Cover and cook, stirring
once or twice, for 30 minutes. Add the sausage and green chiles and cook, uncovered,
stirring often, until very thick, about 45 minutes. Adjust the seasoning.

Spoon the rice into wide bowls, top with the bean mixture, and serve immediately.

New Southwestern Cassoulet

IN THE SOUTHWEST OF FRANCE, ONE OF THE REGIONAL SPECIAL-TIES IS a hearty meat and bean dish called cassoulet. Chili con carne it isn't, but with a few Southwest Texan twists, it is a very satisfying main course, perfect for a company dinner on that first chilly autumn night.

1/4 cup olive oil

1 large (5-pound) young chicken, cut into 8 serving pieces

1/2 pound kielbasa or other cooked smoked sausage, cut into 1/2-inch slices

2 cups chopped yellow onions

3 medium carrots, peeled and sliced

2 bay leaves

6 cups cooked and drained flageolets or great Northern beans

2 1/2 cups lightly salted chicken broth

1 1/2 cups canned crushed tomatoes in purée

1 cup dry white wine

6 garlic cloves, peeled and chopped

1 teaspoon salt

6 long green chiles, roasted, peeled, and chopped (page 41), or 1 cup frozen chopped green chiles, thawed (not drained)

2 1/2 tablespoons minced thyme

1 1/2 cups soft bread crumbs

Position a rack in the lower third of the oven and preheat to 350°F.

In a heavy 5-quart nonreactive Dutch oven over medium heat, warm 2 tablespoons of the oil. Working in batches, pat the chicken pieces dry and cook them in the hot oil, turning them once or twice, until lightly browned, about 10 minutes. Reserve. Add the kielbasa slices to the Dutch oven and cook, stirring once or twice, until lightly browned, about 3 minutes. Reserve.

Add the onions, carrots, and bay leaves to the Dutch oven, lower the heat slightly, and cook, covered, stirring occasionally and scraping the bottom of the pan, for 10 minutes. Return the chicken and kielbasa to the pan. Add the beans, broth, tomatoes, wine, garlic, and salt. Raise the heat and bring to a simmer.

Place the cassoulet in the oven and bake, uncovered, for 1 hour. Stir in the green chiles and thyme. Sprinkle the bread crumbs over the cassoulet; drizzle the crumbs with the remaining olive oil and bake, uncovered, until the crumbs are browned and the cassoulet is saucy but not dry, 30 to 40 minutes.

Let rest on a rack to cool for 10 minutes before serving.

Classic Red Chili Colorado con Carne y Frijoles

MAKES 8 SERVINGS

I HAVE ONE RULE ABOUT CHILI MAKING: DO YOUR OWN THING. I HAVE SEEN CHILI COOKS SQUARE OFF over what should or should not go into the pot, but the hottest controversy is always over adding beans. In my kitchen, and in plenty of other Texas kitchens, the beans go *into* the pot, not alongside the chili. As long as the "bowl of red" is thick, spicy, and otherwise brilliant, the beans don't detract one bit.

3 pounds ground beef, preferably coarse "chili grind" or hand-cut into ¼-inch dice

1 pound hot Italian-style sausage, casings removed and crumbled

1 tablespoon salt

8 jalapeños, stemmed and quartered

9 garlic cloves

⅓ cup rendered bacon fat or olive oil

5 cups finely chopped yellow onions

⅓ cup unblended medium-hot powdered red chiles, preferably from Chimayo or Dixon, New Mexico

2 ½ tablespoons ground cumin, preferably from toasted seeds (page 38)

1 ½ tablespoons dried oregano, crumbled

1 tablespoon dried marjoram, crumbled

1 tablespoon freshly ground black pepper

5 cups lightly salted beef broth

2 cups canned crushed tomatoes in purée

6 long green chiles, roasted, peeled, and chopped (page 41), or 1 cup frozen chopped green chiles, thawed (not drained)

3 tablespoons masa harina (corn tortilla flour) or yellow cornmeal

4 ½ cups cooked and drained beans (cook's choice)

Sour cream, grated cheese, chopped onions, sliced black olives, and diced tomatoes, for garnishes (optional)

In a large skillet over medium heat, combine the beef and sausage. Add the salt and cook, uncovered, stirring often and breaking up any lumps, until the meat is uniformly brown and crumbled, about 15 minutes.

Meanwhile, in a food processor, combine the jalapeños and garlic and process until finely chopped. In a 5 ½- to 6-quart nonreactive Dutch oven over low heat, warm the bacon fat. Add the jalapeño mixture, onions, powdered chiles, cumin, oregano, marjoram, and black pepper. Cover and cook, stirring often and scraping the bottom of the pan, for 15 minutes. *(continued)*

Transfer the beef mixture with any juices to the Dutch oven. Stir in the beef broth and crushed tomatoes. Bring to a simmer, then lower the heat and cook, uncovered, stirring occasionally, for 1 hour. Stir in the green chiles and simmer another 30 minutes, or until very thick. Remove the Dutch oven from the heat and let stand for 5 minutes.

Skim the fat from the surface of the chili, reserving 4 tablespoons. In a small bowl, stir the masa harina into the reserved fat. Add this paste back into the chili. *(The chili can be prepared to this point several days in advance. Cool completely, cover, and refrigerate.)* Stir in the beans and rewarm the chili over low heat, stirring often. Serve hot with the desired garnishes.

Boilermaker Baked Beans

❂

THESE SWEET-AND-TART BAKED BEANS ARE ENLIVENED BY A SHOT OF BOURBON AND A GLASS OF DARK BEER. Be sure that the beans are cooked before baking, as the amount of salt and acidic ingredients in this recipe will stop them from further tenderizing. In Texas we don't do *al dente* beans!

10 $\frac{1}{2}$ cups cooked and drained white beans

2 cups chopped yellow onions

$\frac{1}{2}$ pound thick-sliced bacon, cooked crisp and crumbled, with the drippings

1 12-ounce bottle chili sauce, such as Heinz

1 cup dark beer

$\frac{1}{2}$ cup medium-hot tomato salsa

$\frac{1}{4}$ cup bourbon

$\frac{1}{4}$ cup unsulfured molasses

$\frac{1}{4}$ cup Dijon mustard

3 tablespoons packed dark brown sugar

2 tablespoons Worcestershire sauce

1 tablespoon hot pepper sauce

1 $\frac{1}{2}$ teaspoons salt

Position a rack in the middle of the oven and preheat to 350° F.

In a heavy 5-quart nonreactive pot, combine all the ingredients. Cover the pot and bake the beans for 30 minutes. Uncover, stir, and bake another 30 minutes. Stir again and bake until the sauce has thickened but the beans are not dry, about 35 minutes.

Serve the beans hot, warm, or cold.

Beef and Black Bean Burgers

MAKES 4 SERVINGS

MIXING COOKED BLACK BEANS INTO THE GROUND BEEF FOR THESE BURGERS stretches the beef, adds fiber, and tastes great too!

1 pound ground beef
1 cup cooked and drained black beans
Olive oil

Salt and freshly ground black pepper
4 hamburger buns, split and toasted
Cumin Mayonnaise (recipe follows)

In a bowl, lightly but thoroughly mix together the ground beef and beans. Form into 4 thick patties.

Set a large heavy nonstick skillet over medium heat. Film the pan with olive oil. Add the patties and cook until brown, about 4 minutes. Turn the patties and cook until brown and done to your liking, about 3 minutes for medium rare. Season to taste with salt and pepper.

Place each burger on the bottom of a bun. Add a dollop of mayonnaise, cover with a bun top, and serve immediately.

Cumin Mayonnaise

$^1\!/_2$ cup mayonnaise
1 $^1\!/_4$ teaspoons ground cumin, preferably from toasted seeds (page 38)

2 teaspoons fresh lime juice
2 teaspoons minced lime zest (colored peel)

In a small bowl, whisk together the mayonnaise, cumin, lime juice, and zest. Cover and refrigerate until using.

The Old Switcheroo:
Substituting Bean Types

❋

USING ONE TYPE OF BEAN FOR ANOTHER MAY BE ADVENTUR-
OUS, BUT YOU HAVE TO USE COMMON SENSE to prevent it from
being disastrous.

Let's say you like to make minestrone with cannellini beans, but there's a jar of black
beans sitting in the cupboard, and you're thinking of using them instead. Don't do it!
The finished dish will turn out a dark, inky purple—perfectly edible but uglier than an
armadillo in a bikini. On the other hand, garbanzo beans would not only look and taste
delicious but have an Italian sensibility as well.

Heirloom and boutique beans can be substituted for their supermarket cousins. In
fact, it's a good way to begin cooking with the exotic newcomers. Rattlesnake beans are
obviously related to pintos, so it's a cinch to use them in a pinto bean recipe, probably
without any adjustments. It's tempting to substitute gorgeous big, round, black-and-white
dappled Christmas lima beans for the smaller, oval great Northerns, and it could be
done, but probably with considerably more liquid and seasonings. In recipes in which
the beans are precooked, such as salads, the risks are reduced. Substituting bean types is
like learning to ride a horse—experience will eventually teach you, and although you may
get a little sore in the process, learning will be fun.

Toasting Cumin Seeds

❋

TO AVOID OVERBROWNING THE CUMIN (AND DESTROYING THE
SOUGHT-AFTER NUTTY TASTE), begin with a generous quantity of seeds—
half a cup or so. Place the seeds in a small heavy skillet over low heat and cook, stirring
often, until browned and fragrant (some seeds may pop), 7 or 8 minutes. Remove from
the skillet immediately and cool. Store the toasted seeds in an airtight container and grind
them when needed in an electric spice mill or in a mortar with a pestle.

Epazote: The Bean's Wonder Weed

✻

EPAZOTE, A COMMON, PROLIFIC WEED THAT AGGRAVATES THE PANTS OFF TEXAS GARDENERS, is nonetheless the best friend a pot of beans ever had. Mexican tradition says that the addition of chopped epazote leaves to beans reduces flatulence, which makes epazote a pretty good pal to the cook and guests too. It has a strong medicinal (even petrochemical) taste that must be blended with other ingredients in order not to be blatant. Stir a few chopped leaves into a pot of beans (especially black beans) during the last 30 minutes of cooking, and you will be rewarded with a wonderful, if indefinable, flavor. Dried epazote is found in speciality stores and in natural food stores, packed in tea bags, as it is also reputed to be the perfect tea to soothe an upset stomach.

Roasting Chiles and Sweet Peppers

✻

FIRE-ROASTING CHILES LOOSENS THEIR TOUGH, RATHER INDIGESTIBLE PEELS, partially cooks the flesh, and adds a savory, smoky nuance. Roasted directly on the burner grids of a gas range, the chiles will remain slightly crunchy. Roasted under the broiler or on the kind of stove-top chile-roasting rack that sits over an electric or gas burner, the chiles will be softer.

Pierce the chiles near their stems with the tip of a knife. Roast or broil the chiles, turning them often, until the peels are lightly but evenly charred (the appearance of white ash is a sign the chiles have been overroasted, leading to some loss of flesh). Let the chiles steam in a closed paper bag or in a covered bowl until cool. Rub away the burned peel. Wipe the chiles with paper towels to remove as much of the peel as possible, but avoid rinsing the chiles, which washes away flavor.

Stem and seed the chiles and trim off the inner ribs. Chop or julienne the chiles as needed for the recipe.

Chiles may also be peeled by dipping them briefly into hot (375°F) oil, but this method does not add a smoky flavor. Cover and cook, then peel as directed above.

Grilled Red Chile~Soaked Turkey Cutlet and Refried Bean Tortas

✿

NEIGHBORHOOD RESTAURANTS OFTEN SERVE *TORTAS* AT LUNCHTIME, sandwiches of round hard rolls (called *bolillos*) stuffed with favorite lunchmeats and cheeses, garnished with pickled chiles or onion rings, and often grilled. These spectacular sandwiches aren't everyday fare but would be great on a leisurely afternoon with friends.

2 boneless, skinless turkey breast fillets
  (about 1 1/2 pounds total)
1/2 cup pico de gallo (refrigerated fresh
  salsa) or tomato-based hot salsa
1/2 cup Red Chile Purée (page 58)
1 cup wood smoking chips, preferably
  mesquite, soaked in water for
  at least 30 minutes

4 bolillos or other hard rolls, split
1 1/3 cups refried black beans, homemade
  (page 45) or canned, heated
1 1/3 cups grated Monterey Jack cheese
3/4 cup Guacamole (page 54)
2 small tomatoes cored and sliced
1 1/3 cups shredded romaine lettuce

Cut the turkey breasts across the grain and at a slight angle into 1/2-inch slices. With a meat pounder, flatten the slices to about 1/4 inch thick. In a small bowl, stir together the *pico de gallo* and red chile purée. In a shallow nonreactive dish, combine the turkey slices and *pico de gallo* mixture. Cover and let stand at room temperature for 1 hour.

Light a charcoal fire and let it burn down until the coals are evenly white, or preheat a gas grill (medium). Drain the wood chips and scatter them over the hot coals or lava stones. Position the grill rack about 6 inches above the heat source. When the wood chips are smoking heavily, lay the *bolillos,* cut sides down, on the grill rack and toast them lightly, about 30 seconds. Reserve. Lay the turkey slices on the grill rack. Cover and cook, turning them once, until they are just cooked through while remaining juicy, about 4 minutes total. Remove from the heat.

Spread the bottom half of each *bolillo* with one fourth of the beans. Sprinkle the beans with the cheese, dividing it evenly and using it all. Arrange the warm turkey slices, overlapping them slightly, over the cheese. Top the turkey with the guacamole, tomatoes, and lettuce. Set the sandwich tops in place, flatten them slightly with the palm of your hand, and use a serrated knife to cut them in half. Serve immediately.

"Pot" Beans and Then Refried Beans

MAKES ABOUT 6 SERVINGS OF POT BEANS,
PLUS 6 SERVINGS OF REFRIED BEANS FROM THE LEFTOVERS

PRACTICALLY EVERY MEXICAN FAMILY PUTS ON A POT OF BEANS IN THE MORNING TO SERVE ALL DAY LONG. (The most ambrosial beans are simmered the night before, refrigerated in their pot, and then reheated the next day.) Beans are spooned alongside meat as a side dish or into a bowl for lunch or even served with sausages and tortillas for breakfast. Leftovers are then frugally mashed and fried for an entirely different but equally wonderful dish.

Pot Beans

2 pounds dried pinto beans, picked over

3 quarts water

1 ½ cups chopped yellow onions

¼ pound (4 or 5 strips) thick-sliced
  smoky bacon, chopped

1 tablespoon unblended medium-hot
  powdered red chiles preferably from
  Chimayo or Dixon, New Mexico

3 garlic cloves, peeled and chopped

Salt

In a large bowl, soak the beans in cold water for 15 minutes, changing the water 3 times.

In a large pot (tall rather than wide) combine the rinsed beans, 3 quarts of water, the onions, bacon, powdered chiles, and garlic. Bring to a simmer, then partially cover and cook, stirring occasionally, for 2 hours. Stir in 4 teaspoons salt and cook until the beans are very tender and their broth is very thick, another hour or more. Adjust the seasoning and serve immediately. (*The beans can be prepared several days in advance and will improve upon resting. Cool completely, cover, and refrigerate. Rewarm the beans over low heat, stirring often, until simmering.*)

Refried Beans

2 tablespoons olive oil

6 cups leftover pot beans, with their liquid

Warm the oil in a large nonstick skillet over low heat. Add 1 cup of the beans with liquid and cook, mashing them roughly and stirring often, until thick, about 5 minutes. Repeat, adding beans and liquid 1 cup at a time. The beans are done when they are thick and creamy but not dry. Serve immediately. (*The beans can be refried a few hours in advance. Add the last cup of beans with liquid and immediately remove the skillet from the heat. Partially cover and hold at room temperature. Rewarm over low heat, mashing and stirring until thick and creamy.*)

White Bean Purée with Thyme-Lemon Butter

INVITE YOU TO WHIP UP (LITERALLY) THIS CLASSY PREPARA-
TION THE NEXT TIME you have a hankering for mashed potatoes—it is
terrific with grilled lamb or roast chicken. Your guests will be pleasantly surprised when
they discover it's made from white beans. Some other time, try it with fresh rosemary
instead of thyme.

7 cups cooked and drained cannellini (white
  kidney beans) or great Northern beans
½ cup half-and-half

½ cup chicken broth
1 ¼ teaspoons salt
Thyme-Lemon Butter (recipe follows)

In a food processor, combine the beans, half-and-half, chicken broth, and salt.
Process, stopping once or twice to scrape down the sides of the work bowl, until fairly
smooth. (For an even silkier texture, force the puréed beans through the medium blade of
a food mill.)

In a medium, preferably nonstick saucepan, warm the purée over low heat, stirring
often, until steaming. Serve immediately, passing the butter at the table.

Thyme-Lemon Butter

¾ stick (6 tablespoons) unsalted butter,
  softened
1 tablespoon minced fresh thyme leaves

1 teaspoon minced lemon zest (colored peel)
½ teaspoon freshly ground black pepper
Pinch of salt

In a bowl, mash together all the ingredients. Use immediately. *(The butter can also be
tightly covered and refrigerated for up to 3 days or frozen for up to 1 month. Soften to room
temperature before using.)*

My Texas Caviar

MAKES 6 TO 8 SERVINGS

THE TEXAS TRADITION OF SERVING BLACK-EYED PEA SALAD ON NEW YEAR'S DAY is said to bring good luck and prosperity throughout the year (the black-eyed peas are supposed to represent coins). Here's my newfangled version with grilled tomato dressing. It's a fine salad, but try it as a super-chunky salsa or as a side dish for grilled meats.

3 medium red-ripe tomatoes
   (about 1 1/2 pounds total)
1/2 cup olive oil
1/3 cup sherry vinegar
2 tablespoons fresh lime juice
3 garlic cloves, peeled and chopped

1 1/2 teaspoons salt
6 cups cooked and drained black-eyed peas
1/3 cup diced red onions
1/3 cup finely chopped cilantro
2 medium jalapeños, stemmed and cut
   into thin rounds

Preheat the broiler. In a shallow metal pan, broil the tomatoes, turning them once, until the peels are evenly charred, about 20 minutes total. Cool to room temperature; core the tomatoes.

In a food processor, combine the tomatoes, their peels and any juices, the olive oil, vinegar, lime juice, garlic, and salt and process until smooth. In a large bowl, combine the peas, dressing, onions, cilantro, and jalapeños. Cover and let stand at room temperature for at least 30 minutes before serving. (*The salad can be prepared up to 2 days in advance. Reserve the onions and cilantro, cover, and refrigerate. Return the salad to room temperature and stir in the onions and cilantro just before serving.*)

Rosemary Bean-Vegetable Pot

❀

MAKES 6 SERVINGS

JACOB'S CATTLE (ALSO CALLED ANASAZI) ARE WHITE HEIRLOOM BEANS WITH MAROON SPLOTCHES and have a slightly sweet taste. This long-simmered vegetarian stew can be a side dish, but I serve it as a main course, along with salsa, corn bread, and honey.

1 pound dried Jacob's cattle beans,
   picked over
2 cups chopped yellow onions
1 cup chopped carrots
8 garlic cloves, peeled and chopped
2 bay leaves
6 cups water

2 large ripe tomatoes, chopped, with
   their juices
4 teaspoons minced fresh rosemary
3/4 teaspoon dried epazote (page 41)
4 teaspoons salt
1 1/2 teaspoons freshly ground black pepper

Cover the beans with cold water and let soak for 4 hours.

Preheat the oven to 350°F. Drain the beans. In a heavy 5-quart pot, combine the beans, onions, carrots, garlic, bay leaves, and water. Cover the pot, set it in the oven, and bake for 1 1/2 hours, stirring once or twice.

Add the tomatoes, rosemary, epazote, salt, and pepper and bake, uncovered, stirring once or twice, until the beans are tender and their liquid is thick, about 1 1/2 hours. Adjust the seasoning and serve immediately. *(The beans can be prepared 2 or 3 days in advance. Cool completely, cover, and refrigerate. Rewarm over low heat, stirring often, until steaming.)*

Creamy Poblano Succotash

FOR MOST COOKS, THE WORD SUCCOTASH IS A SYNONYM FOR BORING. Not my renovated succotash—cloaked in a creamy chicken stock sauce and spiced up with roasted poblano chiles. You may want to taste the roasted poblanos for hotness and adjust the amount you use to taste, or use roasted sweet red peppers for a milder version (or if poblanos are hard to locate in your area).

½ stick (4 tablespoons) unsalted butter
2 poblanos, roasted, peeled, and
    chopped (page 41)
½ cup finely chopped yellow onions
2 garlic cloves, minced
2 cups sweet corn kernels and juices, cut
    and scraped from 4 medium ears

2 cups cooked and drained baby lima beans
1 cup heavy whipping cream
⅓ cup lightly salted chicken broth
½ teaspoon salt
2 teaspoons fresh lemon juice

In a large skillet over medium heat, melt the butter. Add the poblanos, onions, and garlic; cover and cook until tender, about 8 minutes. Stir in the corn, lima beans, cream, broth, and salt and bring to a simmer. Cook, uncovered, stirring occasionally, until thick, about 5 minutes. Remove from the heat, stir in the lemon juice, and serve immediately.

Guacamole

MAKES ABOUT 2 CUPS

TWO HINTS FOR MAKING WORLD-CLASS "GWAK." USE THE BLACK, PEBBLY-SKINNED CALIFORNIA (also called Haas) avocados, not the green, thin-skinned ones from Florida. Nicely ripened, they "give" slightly when squeezed—they shouldn't be squishy. And while I like to use a mini processor to make the seasoning purée, I mash the avocados with a fork, as the end result should be chunky, not smooth as baby food.

3/4 cup chopped cilantro
1 1/2 fresh jalapeños, stemmed and
   chopped
3/4 teaspoon salt

3 large ripe California avocados,
   pitted and peeled
3/4 pound (3 or 4) ripe Italian-style
   plum tomatoes, diced
1/3 cup diced yellow or red onions

In a mini food processor, purée together the cilantro, jalapeños, and salt. In a medium bowl, roughly mash the avocados with a fork. Stir in the cilantro purée, tomatoes, and onions. Adjust the seasoning. *(The guacamole can be prepared up to 3 hours ahead. Cover it with plastic wrap, pressing the film onto the surface of the guacamole, and refrigerate.)*

Garlic Pita Crisps

1/3 cup olive oil
4 garlic cloves, peeled and crushed

6 pita breads
Salt and freshly ground black pepper

Combine the olive oil and crushed garlic and let stand for 30 minutes. Preheat the oven to 450°F. Cut each pita into 8 equal wedges and arrange the wedges in a single layer on 2 baking sheets. Generously brush the tops of the wedges with the garlic oil. Sprinkle with salt and pepper. Working in batches, bake the wedges in the middle level of the oven until crisp and brown, about 6 minutes. Cool on paper towels. *(Use immediately, or store in an airtight container at room temperature. The crisps can be made several days in advance; they will get crunchier as they stand.)*

Crema

MAKES ABOUT 2 CUPS

CREMA IS THE TANGY MEXICAN EQUIVALENT OF THE FRENCH CRÈME FRAÎCHE, a thick cream that is similar to our sour cream but won't separate if heated. If you are using crema in a cold dish, you can substitute sour cream, but it won't be quite as good.

2 cups heavy cream, preferably not
ultra-pasteurized

3 tablespoons cultured buttermilk or
plain yogurt

In a bowl, whisk together the heavy cream and buttermilk. Loosely cover and let stand at room temperature for 12 hours; the mixture will thicken and become acidic. Cover and refrigerate until using; the cream will thicken further and become more tart. It will keep for up to 10 days.

Tostaditas

MAKES A PILE OF CHIPS

24 6-inch yellow or blue corn tortillas   Corn or peanut oil, for deep-frying   Salt

Stack the tortillas together a few at a time and, with a long sharp knife, cut them into 6 equal wedges. Spread the tortillas on the work surface for 15 or 20 minutes to dry them slightly.

In an electric deep-fryer or a medium heavy saucepan fitted with a frying thermometer and set over medium heat, warm the oil to between 375° and 400°F. (The fryer or pan should be no more than half full.) Working in batches to avoid overcrowding the fryer, cook the tortilla wedges, stirring them once or twice, until they are crisp but not browned, about 1 minute. With a slotted spoon, transfer the tostaditas to paper towels to drain. Sprinkle them lightly with salt to taste.

Red Chile Purée

DRIED RED CHILES NEED TO BE SOAKED TO RECONSTITUTE THEIR FLESH, then puréed and sieved to remove their tough skins. The resulting crimson paste (which can be refrigerated or frozen) contains the very essence of the chiles, and while not used as is, it is the foundation of many chile-flavored dishes. Here is the method.

6 cups boiling water
¼ pound (about 12 large) mild New
   Mexico red chile pods, stemmed,
   seeded, and torn into small pieces

2 chiles de árbol, stemmed and
   torn into small pieces
1 cup hot tap water

In a medium heat-proof bowl, combine the boiling water with the pieces of chile. Cover and let stand, stirring occasionally, until cool.

Drain, discarding the soaking water. In a food processor, combine the soaked chile pieces with the hot tap water and process, stopping to scrape down the sides of the work bowl once or twice, until smooth.

Transfer the purée to a sieve set over a bowl. With a rubber scraper, force the purée through the sieve into the bowl; discard any tough peels or seeds that remain. *(The purée can be covered and refrigerated for up to 3 days or frozen for up to 2 months.)*

Mail-Order Sources

THE EL PASO CHILE COMPANY
909 Texas Avenue
El Paso, TX 79901
(915) 544-3434
Southwestern ingredients, gifts,
autographed cookbooks

THE BEAN BAG
818 Jefferson Street
Oakland, CA 94607
(800) 845-2326
Boutique and heirloom beans

COYOTE CAFE GENERAL STORE
132 West Water Street
Santa Fe, NM 87501
(800) 866-HOWL
Boutique and heirloom beans

DEAN & DELUCA
560 Broadway
New York, NY 10012
(800) 221-7714
Boutique and heirloom beans

GALLINA CANYON RANCH
P.O. Box 706
Abiquiu, NM 87510
Boutique and heirloom beans and seeds

PHIPPS RANCH
P.O. Box 349
Pescadero, CA 94060
(415) 879-0787
Boutique and heirloom beans

SHEPHERD'S GARDEN SEEDS
30 Irene Street
Torrington, CT 06790
(203) 482-3638
Heirloom bean seeds

VERMONT BEAN SEED COMPANY
Garden Lane
Fair Haven, VT 05743
(802) 273-3400
Boutique and heirloom bean seeds

WALNUT ACRES
Penns Creek, PA 17862
(800) 433-3998
Boutique and heirloom beans

Index

"pot" beans, 45
purée:
    red chile, 58
    white bean, with thyme-lemon butter, 47

Rattlesnake beans, 6
red beans and rice, El Paso, 29
red chili, classic Colorado con carne y
    frijoles, 32-35
red chile purée, 58
refried bean(s), 45
    tortas, with grilled red chile-soaked
    turkey cutlets, 42
sage oil, chickpea soup with grilled
    sausages and, 24

Salads:
    hot and smoky bean-corn with chile-
    roasted chicken, 26
    my Texas caviar, 48
salsas:
    chunky three-bean, 10
    my Texas caviar, 48
sandwiches:
    beef and black bean burgers, 36
    grilled red chile-soaked turkey cutlet
    and refried bean tortas, 42
sausages:
    chickpea soup with grilled sausages and
    green sage oil, 24
    El Paso red beans and rice, 29

new Southwestern cassoulet, 30
scarlet runner beans, 6
side dishes:
    boilermaker baked beans, 35
    creamy poblano succotash, 52
    my Texas caviar, 48
    rosemary bean-vegetable pot, 51
    white bean purée with thyme-lemon
    butter, 47
soups:
    chickpea with grilled sausages and
    green sage oil, 24
    gingered yellow split pea with cilantro
    cream, 23
split pea, yellow gingered soup with
    cilantro cream, 23
succotash, creamy poblano, 52

Texas caviar, my, 48
three-bean salsa, chunky, 10
thyme-lemon butter, for white
    bean purée, 47
tongues-of-fire beans, 6
    hot and smoky bean-corn salad with chile
    roasted chicken, 26
tostaditas, 57
turkey cutlet and refried bean tortas,
    grilled red chile-soaked, 42

White bean purée with thyme-lemon
    butter, 47